D1294122

UNCOVERING THE PAST:
ANALYZING PRIMARY SOURCES

THE SPACE RACE

HEATHER HUDAK

CRABTREE
PUBLISHING COMPANY
WWW.CRABTREEBOOKS.COM

Author: Heather C. Hudak

Editor-in-Chief: Lionel Bender

Editors: Simon Adams, Ellen Rodger

Proofreaders: Laura Booth, Angela Kaelberer

Project coordinator: Petrice Custance

Design and photo research: Ben White

Production: Kim Richardson

**Production coordinator and
   prepress technician:** Ken Wright

Print coordinator: Katherine Berti

Consultant: Amie Wright,
   The New York Public Library

Produced for Crabtree Publishing Company
by Bender Richardson White

Photographs and reproductions:
Alamy: 14 (AF archive), 29, 30 (John Frost Newspapers); Getty Images: 7
(Popular Science), 8–9 (Ralph Morse), 13 (Hulton Archive), 15 Top, 23 Top
(Corbis Historical), 15 Btm, 22 (Archive Photos), 25 (Stringer), 28–29 (CBS), 33
(SSPL), 40–41 (VGC), 41 (Manjunath Kiran/Stringer); John F. Kennedy Library:
10 (John F. Kennedy Library); NASA: 3, 20–21, 28, 31, 32 Left (NASA), Top Left
(Icon) 4, 6 (Kennedy Space Center), 4–5 (Project Apollo), 1, Top Left (Icon) 8, 10,
12, 14, 20, 22, 24, 26, 28, 30, 32 (Marshall Space Flight Center), 9 (Johnson Space
Center), Top Left (Icon) 16, 18 (NASA), 24 (JPL), 32 Rt, Top Left (Icon) 34, 36,
34–35, 37 (JSC); Topfoto: 6, 23 Btm (World History Archive), 11 (SCRSS), 12, 36
(The Granger Collection), 16–17 (Topham Picturepoint), 18 (The Image Works),
19 (Topfoto), 26 (Sputnik/Topfoto), 27 (HIP/Topfoto); Wikimedia.org: front
cover (Jack Weir (1928-2005))

Map: Stefan Chabluk

Cover: Washington Post headline day after NASA's *Apollo 11* lands first
humans on the moon.

Library and Archives Canada Cataloguing in Publication

Hudak, Heather C., 1975-, author
     The space race / Heather Hudak.

(Uncovering the past: analyzing primary sources)
Includes bibliographical references and index.
Issued in print and electronic formats.
ISBN 978-0-7787-4749-9 (hardcover).--
ISBN 978-0-7787-4817-5 (softcover).--
ISBN 978-1-4271-2087-8 (HTML)

     1. Space race--History--Juvenile literature. 2. Space
race--History--Sources--Juvenile literature. 3. Manned space
flight--History--Juvenile literature. 4. Manned space flight--
History--Sources--Juvenile literature. I. Title.

TL788.5.H83 2018   j629.45009   C2017-907711-2
                                                         C2017-907712-0

Library of Congress Cataloging-in-Publication Data

Names: Hudak, Heather C., 1975- author.
Title: The space race / Heather Hudak.
Description: New York, New York : Crabtree Publishing, [2018]
   Series: Uncovering the past : analyzing primary sources |
   Includes bibliographical references and index.
Identifiers: LCCN 2017057599 (print) | LCCN 2017058377 (ebook)
   ISBN 9781427120878 (Electronic) |
   ISBN 9780778747499 (hardcover : alk. paper) |
   ISBN 9780778748175 (pbk. : alk. paper)
Subjects: LCSH: Space race--History--Juvenile literature. |
   Astronautics--United States--History--Juvenile literature. |
   Astronautics--Soviet Union--History--Juvenile literature.
Classification: LCC TL793 (ebook) | LCC TL793 .H795 2018
   (print) | DDC 629.409/046--dc23
LC record available at https://lccn.loc.gov/2017057599

Crabtree Publishing Company
www.crabtreebooks.com   1-800-387-7650

Printed in the U.S.A./022018/CG20171220

Published in Canada
Crabtree Publishing
616 Welland Ave.
St. Catharines, ON
L2M 5V6

Published in the United States
Crabtree Publishing
PMB 59051
350 Fifth Avenue, 59th Floor
New York, NY 10118

Published in the United Kingdom
Crabtree Publishing
Maritime House
Basin Road North, Hove
BN41 1WR

Published in Australia
Crabtree Publishing
3 Charles Street
Coburg North
VIC, 3058

UNCOVERING THE PAST

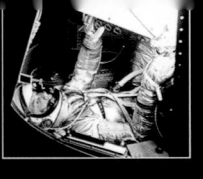

THE PAST COMES ALIVE

"Humanity must rise above Earth, to the top of the atmosphere and beyond, for only thus will we fully understand the world in which we live."

Socrates, Greek philosopher, c. 400 B.C.

The Space Race was an event that happened in the past between the United States and the Soviet Union. Following **World War II**, the two nations became rivals due largely to their vastly different political systems and beliefs about how **societies** should work. The Soviets wanted to spread their **communist** ideals to other nations, which the United States opposed and feared. This time in history became known as the **Cold War**, and it lasted until the early 1990s.

At the start of the Cold War, the two superpowers vied for dominance in the **Arms Race.** One result was the creation of powerful **rockets** that could launch objects into space. In the summer of 1955, the United States declared it would send artificial **satellites** into space in the next few years. A few days later, the U.S.S.R. made a similar decree. The two nations spent nearly two **decades** trying to best each other in the Space Race. They wanted to prove themselves as leaders in the areas of scientific, military, and technical research and development.

Historians are people who study the past. They look for sources of information that provide **evidence** about major events and people in earlier times. They **analyze** and interpret these sources to find out how we can prevent similar events in the future. The Space Race tells us about beliefs and **culture** of the time. It had a major influence on people and politics that continues to shape society today. Many different viewpoints were captured using cameras and other recording devices. In addition, events that took place during the Space Race have been well preserved in interviews, books, posters, movies, and more.

DEFINITIONS

The **Union of Soviet Socialist Republics** (U.S.S.R.) was a communist country in Northern Asia and Eastern Europe that was made up of Russia and 14 other republics or distinct regions. **Soviet** is a term used to describe anything related to the U.S.S.R.

Communism refers to an **economic** and political system in which all property is owned by its members and is used for the good of all people. **Capitalism** refers to an economic and political system in which trade and industry are privately owned.

▲ During the 1960s and 1970s, 12 U.S. astronauts walked on the moon as part of the Apollo program. They are the only people to have walked on the moon to date.

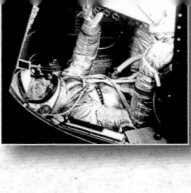
THE FIRST AND SECOND RED SCARES

In Russia in the early 1910s there were strikes, bombings, and labor unrest as workers and peasants became **disillusioned** and tried to overthrow their harsh government. The October **Revolution** of 1917 led to a government run by the Russian Communist Party. It was opposed to **capitalism** and wanted to create a society where everyone was equal. It soon wanted to spread its beliefs to other countries, including the United States and Canada.

Following **World War I,** communist groups started to form in America. Many North Americans began to fear a communist revolution would happen in their own countries, taking away many of the rights and freedoms they enjoyed as part of a democratic society. In a communist country, people cannot own land or businesses, and they are given only what they need to survive. After a series of **strikes** led by communist groups broke out in the United States in 1919, the fear of communism reached a peak. It wasn't long before the U.S. government began to take action, **prosecuting** anyone with communist ties. This period in history is known as the First Red Scare, and it lasted until mid-1920.

Over the next 25 years, government initiatives were put in place to deal with anyone who was believed to be taking part in communist, **subversive**, or "un-American" activities. Tensions between the United States and the Soviet Union once again flared following World War II when they were locked in economic and political battles known as the Cold War.

"If I could get one message to you it would be this: the future of this country and the welfare of the free world depends upon our success in space. There is no room in this country for any but a fully cooperative, urgently motivated all-out effort toward space leadership. No one person, no one company, no one government agency, has a monopoly on the competence, the missions, or the requirements for the space program."

Vice President Lyndon B. Johnson, 1961

PERSPECTIVES

Look at both of the images on this page. What point of view does each represent? How do they compare? How are they different?

During this time, a second wave of communist fears swept through North America. Many people believed the Soviets had planted **spies** in government departments, universities, and other industries. In response, the governments of both Canada and the United States pointed fingers at anyone they believed to have communist **affiliations**. The Second Red Scare peaked in the late 1940s and lasted well into the 1950s.

In the 1950s, the Cold War conflict escalated beyond Earth's atmosphere, as the United States and the U.S.S.R. battled to be the first to conquer outer space. The Soviets launched the first successful satellite, *Sputnik*, in 1957, and then put a man in space in 1961. The Americans were eager to follow suit and quickly ramped up their space program in an attempt to outdo their Soviet rivals. This time in history became known as the Space Race.

▲ A Soviet poster from 1963 shows cosmonaut Valentina Tereshkova, the first woman in space. "Cosmonaut" was the Soviet equivalent of "astronaut."

▶ Magazines such as *Popular Science* featured the Space Race and were designed to get readers excited about space exploration.

7

TYPES OF EVIDENCE

"We are at a point in history where a proper attention to space, and especially near space, may be absolutely crucial in bringing the world together."

Margaret Mead, American anthropologist

Historians have an important job. They look at what caused events to occur and the effect they and the people involved had on society. In some cases, the work historians perform helps prevent societies from making the same mistakes in the future.

In order to get a clear picture of the past, historians need to learn much more than just the details of a specific event. They need to understand what was happening in society at the time. Learning about topics such as culture, economy, politics, and religion is key to uncovering the past. Since historians don't have time machines to go back and experience the past, they need to look for evidence that can help them see the event from the **perspectives** of people who witnessed it firsthand. Evidence consists of any facts or information that can help confirm a claim or belief. It provides proof that certain events took place. Historians analyze, inspect, examine, and decipher evidence to produce an account of the past.

Historians look to **source materials** to provide the evidence they need to draw conclusions and write reports. Source materials are any **artifacts** that were created about the time in history being studied. They can include articles, recordings, books, photographs, paintings, and more.

▶ On March 17, 1960, the Mercury Seven wear their pressure suits at Langley Air Force Base in Virginia to test out equipment they would need in space.

▶ In 1959, **NASA** chose seven people to become the first U.S. astronauts. Known as the Mercury Seven, they were, from left to right, Alan B. Shepard, Jr., Scott Carpenter, Gordon Cooper, Jr., Donald K. Slayton, Virgil Grissom, John Glenn, Jr., and Walter M. Schirra.

▲ *Apollo 11* was the first manned spacecraft to land on the moon. It launched from Kennedy Space Center (KSC), at 9:32 A.M. on July 16, 1969.

PRIMARY SOURCES

If you've ever snapped a selfie of you and your friends at an event, you've created a type of evidence called a **primary source**. Primary sources are any artifacts created by people who personally witnessed or took part in events as they happened. Historians look to as many primary sources as they can. They need many firsthand accounts to create a clear picture of the past.

Historians use primary sources to get a sense of what people were thinking or feeling as events were unfolding. Primary sources often reflect personal experiences or opinions and provide a great deal of insight into the culture and society during a specific period of time. They include anything that can be stored, preserved, and passed down to future **generations**, such as artwork, photographs, recordings, legal documents, interviews, creative writing, laboratory results, and more. Even emails you send to your friends or posts you make on social **media** are types of primary sources that future historians may use as evidence of what life was like for people living in the 21st **century**.

Primary sources are often found in **archives,** museums, and libraries. Some primary sources are available through online databases such as the Library of Congress. Websites like Flickr and Wiki Commons also provide access to primary sources. However, some primary sources are kept in private collections. Others include classified government records that have yet to be released to the public. Historians may find these difficult or impossible to access and study.

THE WHITE HOUSE
WASHINGTON

April 20, 1961

MEMORANDUM FOR

VICE PRESIDENT

In accordance with our conversation I would like for you as Chairman of the Space Council to be in charge of making an overall survey of where we stand in space.

1. Do we have a chance of beating the Soviets by putting a laboratory in space, or by a trip around the moon, or by a rocket to land on the moon, or by a rocket to go to the moon and back with a man. Is there any other space program which promises dramatic results in which we could win?

2. How much additional would it cost?

3. Are we working 24 hours a day on existing programs. If not, why not? If not, will you make recommendations to me as to how work can be speeded up.

4. In building large boosters should we put out emphasis on nuclear, chemical or liquid fuel, or a combination of these three?

5. Are we making maximum effort? Are we achieving necessary results?

I have asked Jim Webb, Dr. Weisner, Secretary McNamara and other responsible officials to cooperate with you fully. I would appreciate a report on this at the earliest possible moment.

"...the United States was not built by those who waited and rested and wished to look behind them. This country was conquered by those who moved forward, and so will space."

U.S. President John F. Kennedy, 1962

▲ On April 20, 1961, President John F. Kennedy wrote a memo to Vice President Lyndon B. Johnson about the state of the national space program.

Written primary sources include:

- Diaries: Notebooks people use to write down their personal thoughts and experiences
- Autobiographies: Books people write about their own life experiences
- Reports: Formal written or spoken statements about something a person has seen, heard, done, or examined
- Essays: Short pieces of writing through which the writer expresses an opinion or theory about a specific subject
- Blogs: Websites where people share their personal experiences or thoughts
- Lyrics: The words to a poem or a song

The Space Race is well documented in primary sources such as newspaper articles, transcripts of speeches, and government reports. There are even telegrams and memos between political leaders like President John F. Kennedy, Vice President Lyndon B. Johnson, and Soviet **Premier** Nikita Khrushchev.

At the time of the Space Race, many primary sources were sealed from the public. They contained sensitive information such as top-secret scientific designs that the U.S. government did not want the Soviets to know about. Many of these sources can be viewed now.

ANALYZE THIS

Read the memorandum from President Kennedy to Vice President Johnson. What perspective does Kennedy represent? Does he express any concerns? What point is he trying to make?

▼ Crowds of people gathered in the Soviet Union to read about cosmonaut Yuri Gagarin becoming the first human in orbit on April 12, 1961.

PERSPECTIVES

What can you tell about how the people in the photograph are feeling? Why do you think they are all gathered in one place? What does this image tell you about Yuri Gagarin's flight into space?

VISUAL AND AUDITORY SOURCES

There's a reason for the saying, "A picture is worth a thousand words." Visual primary sources, such as photographs, give us a glimpse into a particular period of time. They show us people's reactions to certain events, how people dressed, what buildings looked like, and other visual clues into society and everyday life of the time.

Auditory sources of evidence are also valuable tools historians can use to learn more about the past. They include radio interviews and recorded speeches.

▼ On October 5, 1957, the cover of *The New York Times* featured a story about the Soviet launch of the world's first artificial satellite in space, *Sputnik 1.*

Auditory sources give us a sense of what people are thinking and how they are feeling that we might not be able to tell from a picture or drawing. We can hear crowds booing in reaction to an event, the roar of rockets as a satellite launches, or the sobs of someone who is hurt.

Visual and auditory sources of evidence can include:

■ Political cartoons: Drawings that express the opinion of the artist
■ Posters: Large printed pictures that are used to promote goods, services, and ideas
■ Videos: Recordings of moving images
■ Artwork: Paintings, drawings, and sculptures
■ Photographs: Pictures taken with a camera

- Speeches: Addresses people make to express their thoughts to an audience
- Radio interviews: Conversations between a reporter and a witness
- Music recordings: Songs with words about an event or music of the time period
- Oral histories: Recordings of people who have personal experiences with events

During the Space Race, the media was on location for every major event. Radio and television interviews with astronauts such as Neil Armstrong and Buzz Aldrin and live footage of satellites and spacecraft being launched into orbit are examples of visual and auditory evidence created at the time.

The Soviets created many posters during the Space Race as **propaganda** to create excitement about the country's space program. In the United States, political cartoonists such as Herbert Block used humor to showcase events from a political perspective.

EVIDENCE RECORD CARD

Signed publicity portrait photo of cosmonaut Yuri Gagarin

LEVEL Primary source
MATERIAL Color photograph
LOCATION Soviet Union
DATE 1957
SOURCE Universal History Archive/UIG via Getty

PERSPECTIVES

What does *The New York Times* front page tell you about events that were happening in the world at the time? Why is it important to note that the satellite had been seen over the United States? How do you think this headline made Americans feel?

▲ Much like a medal-winning Olympian, Yuri Gagarin was celebrated as a hero after becoming the first human in space.

ADDITIONAL SOURCES OF EVIDENCE

Secondary sources are types of evidence that are created after an event has occurred. People who create secondary sources did not personally witness or experience the particular period in history. Instead, they acquired secondhand knowledge of it by analyzing and interpreting primary sources.

Books, movies, paintings, biographies, and reconstructions based on primary sources are examples of secondary sources. Together, they give different perspectives and viewpoints on events. In creating secondary sources, it is often easy to remove personal opinions from accounts and to give a **balanced** story. Although this evidence is probably not as **accurate** or reliable as primary sources, it is invaluable to historians.

There are many Hollywood movies based on real-life events that happened during the Space Race. The 1995 hit movie *Apollo 13* told the true story of three astronauts who were stranded in space after their mission to the moon went wrong. In 2016, the movie *Hidden Figures* relayed the true story of a team of African-American women who worked behind the scenes as mathematicians at NASA during the Space Race.

▲ Tom Hanks played the role of an astronaut stuck in space in the movie *Apollo 13*.

ANALYZE THIS

Why are secondary sources important? How are they different from primary sources? What can a movie like *Apollo 13* tell us about history?

"They turned their desks into a trigonometric war room, poring over equations, scrawling ideas on blackboards, evaluating their work, erasing it, starting over."

— From Margot Lee Shetterly's *Hidden Figures: The American Dream and the Untold Story of the Black Women Mathematicians Who Helped Win the Space Race*

Other examples of secondary sources include magazine articles, Soviet exhibitions promoting space, science-fiction stories, and fact-based television and radio programs. Several nations have even made commemorative pins and postage stamps showcasing key people and major events in the space race, including Soviet cosmonaut Yuri Gagarin and the U.S. lunar landing.

Tertiary sources are made by summarizing both primary and secondary sources of evidence. Encyclopedias, textbooks, almanacs, record books, indexes, and other reference materials that provide an overview of a topic are all examples of tertiary sources.

18 МАРТА 1965 ГОДА ЧЕЛОВЕК ВЫШЕЛ В ПРОСТОРЫ ВСЕЛЕННОЙ.

▲ A Soviet postcard of the first space walk by cosmonaut Alexei Leonov on March 18, 1965.

PERSPECTIVES

Who was the intended audience for this toy? Why would children want to play with toy spacecraft? What does the packaging tell you about the toy?

▼ At the height of the Space Race, many children had toys featuring astronauts like the ones who took part in Project Gemini.

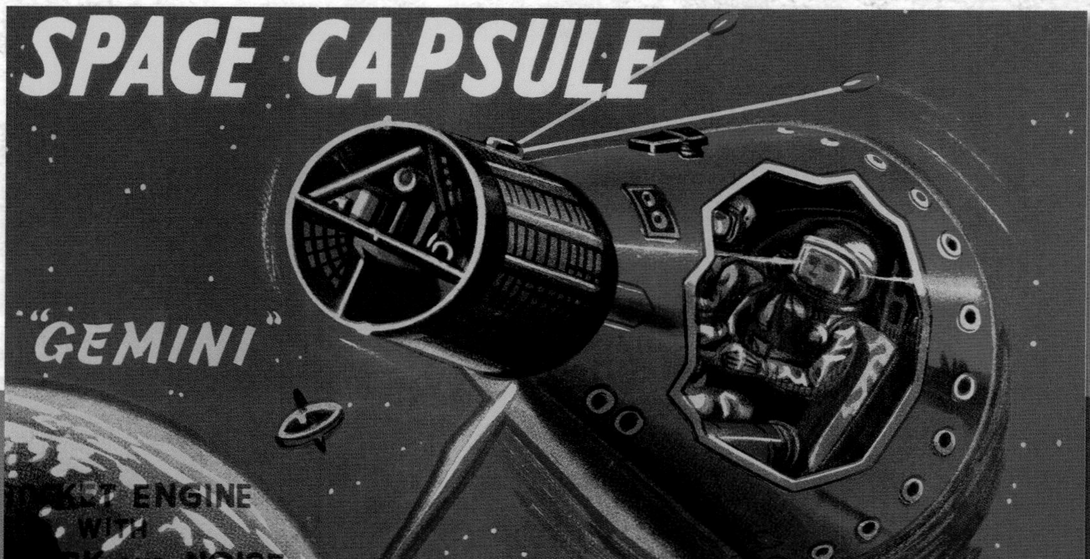

SPACE CAPSULE

"GEMINI"

ROCKET ENGINE
WITH
...CK AND NOISE

FRICTION POWERED

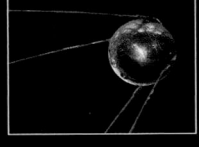
INTERPRETATION

"From now on, we live in a world where man has walked on the moon. And it's not a miracle, we just decided to go."

Jim Lovell, NASA astronaut on *Apollo 13*

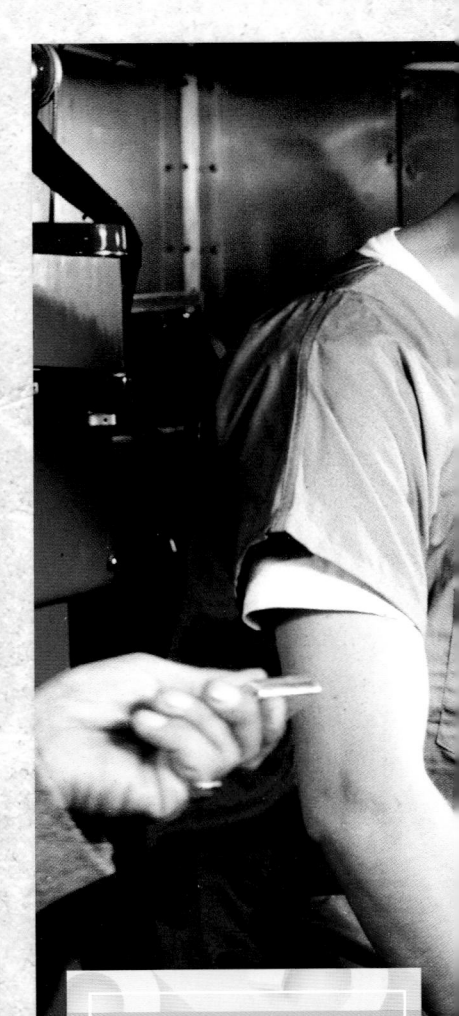

In order to gain insight into the past, historians need to determine if the sources they've acquired are valid, useful, and accurate. To do this, they may look at the **credentials** of the person or organization that created each source, when the source was made or published, and who made the source available. They also look at the point of view each source represents and whether or not it is **biased,** or unbalanced, to try to change someone's perspective on a topic.

Bias happens when there is a clear show of support for or against something. To some extent, all sources are biased. They are shaped and influenced by the events happening in the world at the time they are created. Some people purposely include bias in their source materials. Others include it accidentally. Historians try to look for fact-based sources that are balanced and allow them to see all sides of a story. These are things historians look for that indicate if a source is biased:

- Omitted facts
- Positive or negative word choices
- Additional, unnecessary details
- Extreme language
- Emotional connections
- Political views of the creator

What bias might people have when looking at evidence of the Space Race? Think about the Soviet perspective versus the U.S. perspective and how the biases of each nation may have impacted the sources they created.

PERSPECTIVES

Why were animals sent into space before humans? What can you tell about the animals and the space technicians by looking at these images? Do you think they were happy, excited, or fearful?

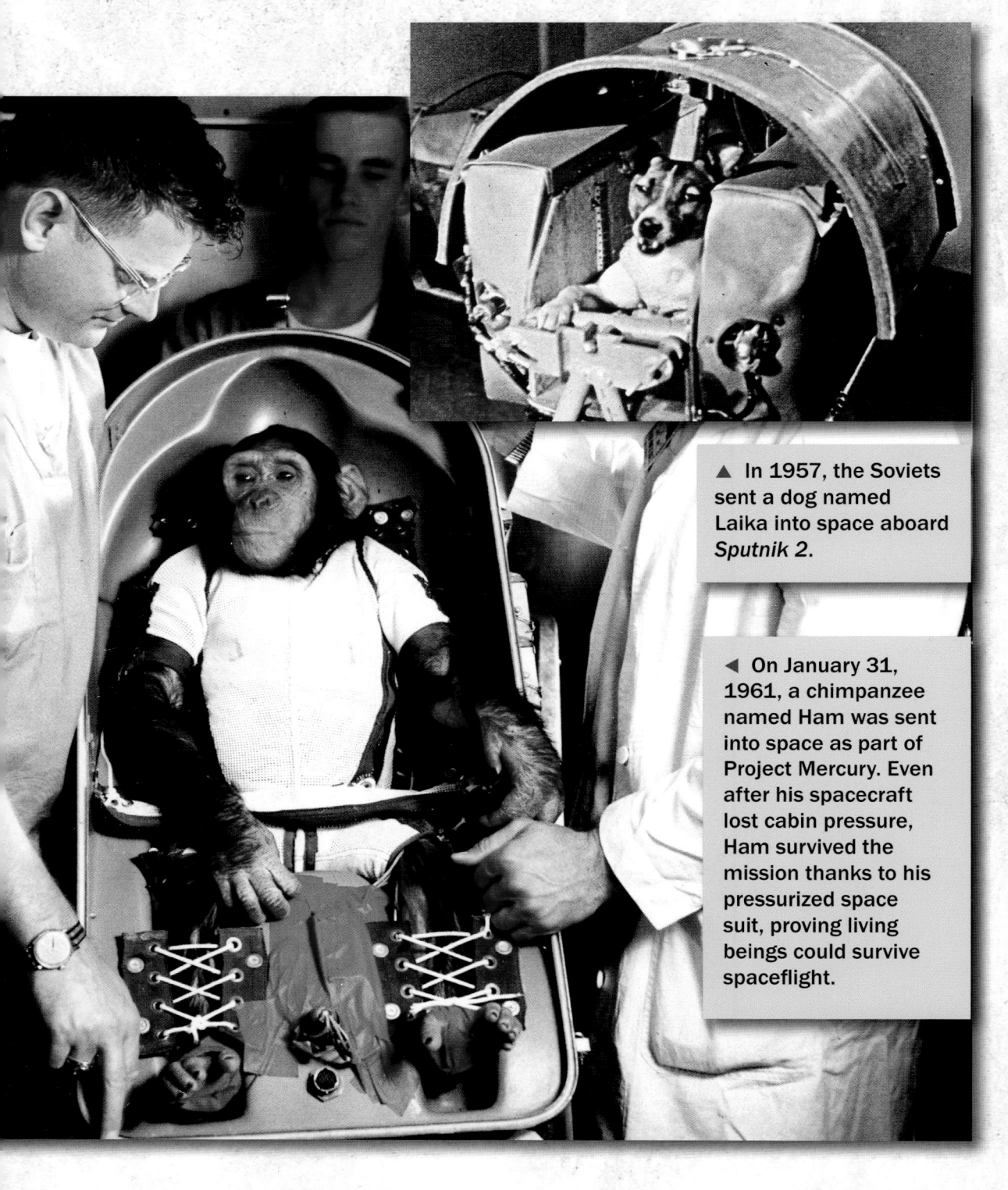

▲ In 1957, the Soviets sent a dog named Laika into space aboard *Sputnik 2*.

◄ On January 31, 1961, a chimpanzee named Ham was sent into space as part of Project Mercury. Even after his spacecraft lost cabin pressure, Ham survived the mission thanks to his pressurized space suit, proving living beings could survive spaceflight.

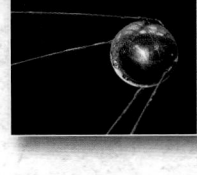

ANALYZING BIAS

Historians take great care to analyze and **evaluate** different sources to ensure they include information essential for their research. Factors they consider when interpreting a source include:

- What type is it—image, transcript—and what evidence does it provide?
- Who created it—is this person **credible**?
- How did the creator get the information such as dates, places, and names?
- Was it created during or after the event?

- What was going on in the world at the time it was created—does it impact the creator's point of view?

Compare different sources. Do they have similar facts and information? Do they have opposing or contradictory place names, dates, and viewpoints? Sometimes people who witness events firsthand misinterpret their experiences. Two people who experience the exact same event, such as a politician giving a speech, may have very different perspectives on the proceedings. They are influenced by their personal beliefs, age, social status, hopes, and fears, for example. They may also be influenced by other events that are happening in the world at the same time. Sometimes different historians come to different conclusions about the past even though they use the same sources.

PERSPECTIVES

Look at the artwork of the Minuteman **missile**. Who is the intended audience? Why do you think the missile is tearing through a Soviet flag? What point of view do you think the artist represents? Do you think the artist was American or Soviet? In what ways might Americans and Soviets feel differently about the artwork?

◀ Minuteman **missiles** were powerful nuclear weapons that could be launched from underground facilities in the United States.

When the Space Race started at the end of World War II, the United States and the Soviet Union had very different views on government and society as a whole. This impacted how their space programs were recorded. In the United States, every rocket launch, satellite mission, and test flight was seen and written up as a victory for a capitalist way of life. In a parallel way, the U.S.S.R. heralded identical space achievements as fine examples of how communism was the way to run a nation. The Soviets tended to report missions only when they had been successful and tried to cover up failed missions. Source materials created during this time were influenced by Cold War tensions and the strong competition between the U.S.S.R. and the United States.

◀ The Soviets displayed missiles and nuclear weapons during the 1962 May Day parade in Red Square, Moscow.

"No nation which expects to be the leader of other nations can expect to stay behind in this race for space...We choose to go to the moon in this decade and do the other things, not because they are easy, but because they are hard."

John F. Kennedy, from his address at Rice University, Texas, September 12, 1962

THE SPACE RACE

"Space travel is life-enhancing, and anything that's life-enhancing is worth doing. It makes you want to live forever."

Ray Bradbury, science-fiction writer, 1920–2012

From the start of World War II, both the Soviets and the Americans battled to build bigger, better nuclear weapons. They were fearful Nazi Germany might develop and perfect the technology before they did. As the war was winding down, Nazi Germany unveiled an **arsenal** of V2 rocket-powered missiles in a last-ditch effort to rise up against the **Allies**. By the end of the war in 1945, the United States and the U.S.S.R. each aimed to get their hands on this new German rocket technology, as well as the scientists and researchers behind it. On May 2, 1945, V2 inventor German scientist Wernher von Braun surrendered to the United States, and the Soviets took control of the V2 factory.

Both nations quickly got to work examining the V2 technology, building their own missiles, and trying to beat each other to the ultimate weapon. The Americans and the Soviets soon realized rocket power had the potential to launch objects into space as well as for military use. The countries became locked in a technological battle.

Starting in the late 1940s, many nations took a keen interest in learning more about space with the goal of bettering the lives of their **citizens**. Only national governments could afford the types of equipment and huge research teams required to run a space-exploration program. In particular, the Soviet and U.S. governments began to invest heavily in space research. The Space Race was a continuation of the rivalry between the two nations in their political systems and their nuclear arms capabilities.

▼ On September 12, 1962, President John F. Kennedy delivered a speech about U.S. space exploration at Rice Stadium in Houston, Texas.

ANALYZE THIS

What do you think were the common beliefs of U.S. society about the Space Race at the time this photo was taken? Were they realistic? How did President Kennedy shape those beliefs?

EVIDENCE RECORD CARD

U.S. President Kennedy gives the "We choose to go to the moon" speech

LEVEL Primary source
MATERIAL Color photograph
LOCATION Houston, Texas
DATE September 12, 1962
SOURCE NASA

ROCKETING INTO SPACE

When the Soviets tested their first atomic bomb in 1949, it took the world by surprise. President Harry S. Truman soon revealed that a German physicist, Klaus Fuchs, who had worked on the first U.S. atomic bombs, had provided details of the technology to the Soviets. Fueled by the fear of a communist takeover, the United States **redoubled** its efforts to outdo the Soviets.

The competition between the two nations resulted in the creation of the hydrogen bomb, strategic bombers, and **intercontinental ballistic missiles**. Each nation equated superiority in politics and economy with its successes in the Space Race, a feeling that was bolstered by the proud sense of **patriotism** that accompanied each achievement.

Advances in rocket technology paved the way for space exploration. Now there was a means for launching objects beyond Earth's atmosphere. In July 1955, the United States announced plans to launch a small satellite into space from July 1, 1957, to December 31, 1958, as part of the **International Geophysical Year**. Just four days later, the Soviets announced their plan to also put a satellite into space in the near future. The race was on. Over the next two years,

EVIDENCE RECORD CARD

Wernher von Braun and President Kennedy at Cape Canaveral

LEVEL Primary source
MATERIAL Photograph
LOCATION Florida, U.S.
DATE November 16, 1963
SOURCE NASA

◀ German-born rocket scientist Wernher von Braun toured Cape Canaveral, Florida, with President John F. Kennedy to publicize the U.S. space program.

both nations worked to build better, more powerful rockets. In the United States, von Braun worked closely with William Pickering, director of the Jet Propulsion Laboratory (JPL), and physicist James A. Van Allen to develop the rocket technology needed to send a satellite into space.

In the Soviet Union, chief engineer Sergei Korolev was the brains behind the world's first intercontinental ballistic missile with a 4,350-mile (7,001-km) range, which he debuted in 1953. Known as the R-7, it had the power to put a satellite into space. Finally, on October 4, 1957, the Soviets used the R-7 to send the *Sputnik 1* satellite into orbit. Again, the world watched in awe as the Soviets took the lead in the Space Race.

◀▼ In the late 1940s, U.S. rocket researchers tested V2 rockets brought from Germany at the White Sands Proving Ground in New Mexico. They became the first-known artificial objects from Earth to reach outer space. Diagrams were used to show the parts of the rocket and to understand how the missile worked.

MISSILE THAT OUTWITTED CONTEMPORARY METHODS OF DEFENCE—THE GERMAN V2 ROCKET-BOMB

4 EXTERNAL CONTROL VANES ① ② COMBUSTION CHAMBER & VENTURI ③ ④ TURBINE & PUMP ASSEMBLY ⑤ ⑥ LIQUID OXYGEN TANK ⑦ ALCOHOL TANK ⑧ CONTROL COMPARTMENT ⑨ ⑩ WARHEAD

4 INTERNAL CONTROL VANES

⑱ ⑰ ⑯ ⑮ ⑭ ⑬ ⑫ ⑪

⑲

㉖ ㉕ ㉔ ㉓ ㉒ ㉑ ⑳

4 STABILIZING FINS

㉙ ㉘ ㉗

1. Chain drive to external control vanes
2. Electric motor.
3. Burner cups.
4. Alcohol supply from pump.
5. Air bottles.
6. Rear joint ring and
7. Servo-operated alcohol outlet valve.

strong point for transport.
8. Nose with device for operating warhead fuse.
9. Radio equipment.
10. Pipe linking alcohol tank and warhead.
11. Nose with device for operating warhead fuse.
12. Conduit carrying wires to 11.

13. Central exploder tube
14. Electric fuze for warhead.
15. Plywood frame.
16. Nitrogen bottles.
17. Front joint ring and strong point for transport.
18. Pitch & azimuth gyros.
19. Alcohol filling point.
20. Alcohol delivery pipe to pump.
21. Oxygen filling point.
22. Concertina connexions.

. Rocket shell construction.

23. Hydrogen peroxide tank.
24. Frame holding turbine and pump assembly.
25. Permanganate tank (gas generator unit behind).
26. Oxygen distributor from pump.
27. Alcohol pipes for subsidiary cooling.
28. Alcohol inlet to double wall.
29. Electro hydraulic Servo motors

"The American and Russian capabilities in space science and technology mesh; they interdigitate. Each is strong where the other is weak. This is a marriage made in heaven—but one that has been surprisingly difficult to consummate."

From Carl Sagan's book *Pale Blue Dot: A Vision of the Human Future in Space*

SOVIETS IN THE LEAD

Radio operators around the world listened for the distinctive beeping sound *Sputnik 1* made as it orbited Earth. Weighing nearly 190 pounds (86 kg), the satellite was the size of a beach ball and had four antennas that looked like whiskers sticking out its side. It traveled at a speed of 17,000 miles per hour (27,359 km/h), orbiting around Earth once every 96 minutes. After 21 days in space, *Sputnik 1* went silent.

Though the satellite had a short life, it had a big impact on the world.

It bolstered global confidence in the Soviet space program and the idea that the U.S.S.R. was ready to explore beyond Earth's atmosphere. On the flipside, the Americans hadn't anticipated the Soviet satellite launch, and many saw it as a sign that the Soviet space program was significantly more advanced than their own. Others feared it was just the first step toward the Soviets using their advanced rocket technology to launch ballistic missiles at the United States. Either way, there was an immediate sense of urgency among Americans to

▲ NASA's Jet Propulsion Laboratory served as mission control for spacecraft. Engineers used a variety of sophisticated technology to monitor the flow of data from spacecraft.

ANALYZE THIS

Why do you think the American people were so concerned about the *Sputnik 1* launch? What was going on in the United States at the time that might have contributed to their fears? How do you think the Soviet people felt about the launch?

"The Russian people had many problems in day-to-day life, they were not too concerned about the first man on the moon."

Sergei Khrushchev, son of Nikita Khrushchev, the Soviet prermier at the height of the Space Race

get their own satellite in space. Still, President Dwight D. Eisenhower refused to panic. He downplayed the importance of the event by calling *Sputnik 1* "one small ball in the air" while putting large amounts of additional funding into the U.S. space program.

Less than a month after *Sputnik 1* made headlines, the Soviets shocked the world once again when they sent a second spacecraft into orbit. On November 3, 1957, *Sputnik 2* hurtled into space carrying a 13-pound (6-kg)

part-Samoyed terrier named Laika. The small dog was outfitted with electrodes to monitor her vital signs of life and send data back to ground control. Since there was no way to bring spacecraft safely back to Earth, the Soviets equipped *Sputnik 2* with enough food, water, and oxygen for Laika to survive 10 days in orbit. However, she died only a day or two into the mission. As the first living being in space, Laika provided invaluable feedback about the impact of space travel on living organisms.

▲ The *Sputnik 1* launch was featured on the front page of the Soviet newspaper *Pravda* on October 6, 1957. The cartoon image shows the world listening for the satellite's beeping sound.

EVIDENCE RECORD CARD

Soviet newspaper featuring *Sputnik 1* launch

LEVEL Primary source
MATERIAL Newspaper
LOCATION Moscow, U.S.S.R.
DATE October 6, 1957
SOURCE AFP/Getty Images

THE UNITED STATES CATCHES UP

Despite public perception, while the Soviets were working on their plans for the R-7 and *Sputnik* satellites, the Americans had, in fact, been busy developing their own rocket and satellite systems. Soon, plans were put in place for a public satellite launch that would show the world exactly what the Americans had been working on.

On December 6, 1957, the U.S. government attempted to use the Vanguard TV3 rocket to launch a 3-pound (1.4-kg) satellite into space, but the result was disastrous. With the world watching on live television, the Vanguard rocket roared to life, lifting about 4 feet (122 cm) off the ground before losing thrust. As it crashed back to Earth, the rocket exploded, causing a great deal of damage to the launch pad and rendering the satellite useless. The media called the Project Vanguard failure "Flopnik" and "Kaputnik," but the U.S. government refused to falter.

Several U.S. rocket and satellite programs had been in the works at the same time. The Martin Company, a

◀ The Baikonur Cosmodrome in a deserted area of Kazakhstan was built in the 1950s for testing Soviet military missiles and spacecraft. *Sputnik 1* was launched from the facility in 1957.

ANALYZE THIS

Why do you think women like Barbara Paulson (page 27) did not receive recognition for their work on the *Explorer 1* mission? What types of jobs did women typically do in the 1960s?

"To be the first to enter the cosmos, to engage, single-handed, in an unprecedented duel with nature—could one dream of anything more?"

Yuri Gagarin, Russian Cosmonaut and the first human to travel into space private **aerospace** organization, had been contracted to lead Project Vanguard. At the same time, von Braun was hard at work on improving his own rocket technology, the Jupiter-C. President Eisenhower had chosen the Vanguard as the first rocket to launch a satellite into space because he hoped to put the focus of the mission on exploring beyond Earth's atmosphere rather than building more powerful weapons technology. However, following the explosion, Eisenhower decided to try von Braun's more powerful Jupiter-C rocket technology for the next launch. Von Braun's team worked in secrecy for months to prepare.

On January 31, 1958, the *Explorer 1* satellite was carried into space by Juno 1, a Jupiter-C rocket. Behind the scenes at the Jet Propulsion Laboratory (JPL) in Pasadena, California, a team of scientists worked tirelessly to ensure the success of the mission. Many of the key players were women who received little recognition for their contributions to the mission. In fact, it was a team of female scientists who calculated the trajectory of *Explorer 1* as it soared into orbit. Barbara Paulson, a 30-year-old woman who had been working at mission control for about 10 years, plotted data coming in from the satellite to confirm it had become the first U.S. artificial satellite in space.

▼ Cosmonaut Yuri Gagarin (left) was the face of the Soviet space program, but Sergei Korolev (right) was the brains behind the technology.

THE SOVIETS LEAP AHEAD AGAIN

With the playing field once again level, President Eisenhower declared on April 2, 1958, Americans would be the first to send a human into orbit. The declaration was quickly followed by signing the National Aeronautics and Space Act into effect on July 29, creating the National Aeronautics and Space Administration (NASA) out of the former National Advisory Committee for Aeronautics. A little more than a year later, NASA took over all U.S. Army space-related projects.

NASA had a budget of more than $100 million and a team of about 8,000. These included astronauts—the "stars" and face of the space program—plus engineers, designers, accountants, doctors, and human computers—mostly women—who performed mathematical calculations by hand before electronic computers were widely available. People all over the world aspired to be involved in the Space Race, and children dreamed of one day exploring space.

Within the space program in the U.S.S.R., Korolev increased the power

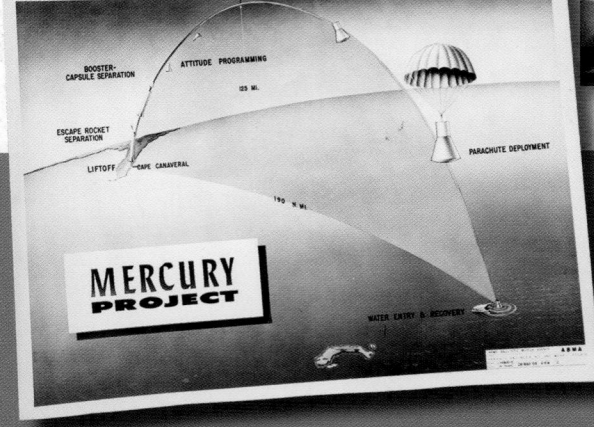

▲ CBS News captured the moment astronaut Alan B. Shepard, Jr. emerged from the *Freedom 7* capsule after parachuting back to Earth on May 5, 1961. Shepard spent 15 minutes and 28 seconds in space.

◄ Illustrations showed the trajectory of the *Freedom 7* capsule that carried astronaut Alan Shepard on his historic flight as the first American in space.

"The United States now sleeps under a Soviet moon."

Nikita Khrushchev

of the R-7 rocket with the goal of launching a payload to the moon. After several failed attempts, the Soviets managed to send the *Luna 2* spacecraft to the moon on September 14, 1959. *Luna 3* flew by the moon nearly a month later, sending pictures back to Earth. It was a major achievement in the Space Race.

Not to be outdone by the Soviets, NASA was busy working on Project Mercury, which aimed to put humans into space aboard a capsule that held only one person at a time. In 1959, NASA chose seven people to train for the Mercury missions. Known as the Mercury Seven, Alan B. Shepard, Jr., Scott Carpenter, Gordon Cooper, Jr., Donald K. Slayton, Virgil Grissom, John Glenn, Jr., and Walter M. Schirra were the nation's first astronauts, and they spent the next several years preparing to travel beyond Earth's atmosphere.

▼ Newspapers across the United States celebrated John Glenn's return to Earth after becoming the first American in orbit.

SUCCESSFUL MANNED SPACEFLIGHT

With the Soviets taking the lead on satellites and spacecraft, it became clear that they would likely be first to send a human into space. This prediction became reality on April 12, 1961, when Yuri Gagarin, one of 200 Russian air force fighter pilots chosen to become cosmonauts, made a single orbit around Earth in a spacecraft called *Vostok 1*. He was celebrated as a hero in the Soviet Union and traveled the world as a "star."

To test the viability of Project Mercury, NASA successfully sent a rhesus monkey named Sam and two chimpanzees named Ham and Enos into space on separate flights aboard Mercury capsules. Finally, on May 5, 1961, *Freedom 7* took off carrying astronaut Alan Shepard. Though he did not reach orbit, Shepard was celebrated as the first American in space (see page 28). In July 1961, another member of the Mercury Seven team, Virgil Grissom, was sent into space on board another Mercury spacecraft, *Liberty Bell 7*.

Over the next several months, the United States and the U.S.S.R. continued to send men into space. In August, the Soviets launched a second man into orbit aboard *Vostok 2*. In February 1962 another of the U.S. Mercury Seven team lifted off. As he soared through space on *Friendship 7*, John Glenn became the first American in orbit. NASA launched three more Project Mercury missions before switching its focus to Project Gemini, which looked at the effects of spaceflight on humans.

As the Soviets worked on rockets that would reach the moon, NASA also made progress in this area. The U.S. *Ranger* program was started in 1959 with the goal of sending spacecraft to the moon. After two failed attempts, *Ranger 3* finally launched on January 26, 1962, but it missed the moon. Several other *Ranger* spacecraft reached the moon but failed to return any data to Earth. The first successful mission to the moon was *Ranger 7*, bringing the Americans a step closer to putting a man on the moon.

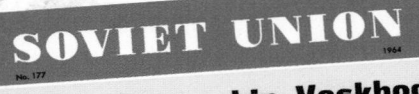

VLADIMIR KOMAROV, KONSTANTIN FEOKTISTOV, AND BORIS YEGO-ROV, THE CREW OF THE SPACESHIP VOSKHOD (SUNRISE) WHO SAW THE SUNRISE 16 TIMES. A START HAS BEEN MADE FOR LONGER FLIGHTS AND BIGGER CREWS IN SPACESHIPS CARRYING OUT MORE DETAILED PROGRAMMES OF RESEARCH. AS BEFORE, THE SOVIET UNION IS GREATLY CONCERNED THAT OUTER SPACE BE USED PURELY FOR PEACE-FUL PURPOSES, AND FOR RESEARCH WHICH WILL BENEFIT HUMANITY

◄ The *Voskhod 1* spacecraft had a three-person crew, as this Soviet propaganda magazine reports. It was the first multiperson space vehicle. Launched on October 13, 1964, it stayed in space for almost two days.

"The dream of yesterday is the hope of today and the reality of tomorrow."

Robert Goddard, U.S. rocket scientist, 1930s

▲ On June 3, 1965, Astronaut Edward H. White II became the first American to walk in space when he stepped outside the *Gemini 4* spacecraft. Soviet cosmonaut Alexei Leonov had made the first spacewalk on March 18, 1965.

THE FIRST PEOPLE ON THE MOON

In 1961, President John F. Kennedy declared the United States would put a man on the moon by the end of the decade. Project Mercury had proved the United States could put humans in space. Project Gemini tested what happened to people when they spent a prolonged period of time there. It also determined if people could venture outside their spacecraft and if they could connect two spacecraft together while in orbit. Canadian aircraft engineer Jim Chamberlin designed the two-person Gemini capsule. In total, there were 12 Gemini missions from 1964 to 1966, but only 10 contained people.

In the same period, the Soviets were busy building newer, better spacecraft, starting with the *Voskhod*. A ramped-up version of the *Vostok*, the *Voskhod 1* was used for two missions in 1964, and *Voskhod 2* flew on two missions in 1965.

In 1967 NASA implemented the *Apollo* program, which was intended to put a human on the moon. *Apollo* spacecraft

▶ Astronaut Neil Armstrong snapped a photo of Buzz Aldrin as he climbed down the ladder of the Lunar Module to take his first steps on the moon.

▼ NASA designed an emblem for Apollo missions. The *Apollo 11* Lunar Module was known as *Eagle*.

"To most people in the UK, indeed throughout Western Europe, space exploration is primarily perceived as 'what NASA does'. This perception is—in many respects—a valid one. Superpower rivalry during the Cold War ramped up US and Soviet space efforts to a scale that Western Europe had no motive to match."

Sir Martin Rees, British space scientist born in 1942

had three components: the Command Module, which had room for three people to fly to the moon and back; the Lunar Module, to carry the astronauts from the Command Module to the moon's surface; and a two- or three-stage Saturn rocket to launch the spacecraft.

The crew of the first manned Apollo mission in 1968 was killed when a fire swept through their cabin a month before the planned launch date. As a result, *Apollo 8* was the first manned mission to the moon. It circled the moon and returned to Earth.

During this time, Canada joined the Space Race. On September 29, 1962, the *Alouette-I* satellite was launched, making Canada the third nation in the world to design and develop an artificial satellite. Scientists at Canada's Defence Research Telecommunications Establishment (DRTE) teamed with NASA to develop the satellite, which would monitor

Earth's **ionosphere**. The partnership went on to include the launch of three more Canadian-made satellites, *Alouette-II* in 1965, *ISIS I* in 1969, and *ISIS II* in 1970.

As the Americans worked on the Apollo design, the Soviets developed the Soyuz spacecraft. However, Korolev's unexpected death early in 1966 left the U.S.S.R.'s space program floundering. Still, the first unmanned Soyuz mission took place in October 1966. In April 1967, a manned crew was launched into space, but a parachute failure upon landing resulted in the death of a cosmonaut. The first successful mission took place in 1968 with *Soyuz 3*.

Finally, on July 20, 1969, the United States accomplished its goal of landing a person on the moon. Millions of people around the world watched in awe as *Apollo 11*'s Neil Armstrong and Buzz Aldrin took their first steps on the moon.

▼ From 1957 to 1966, Sergei Korolev designed a variety of Soviet space launch vehicles.

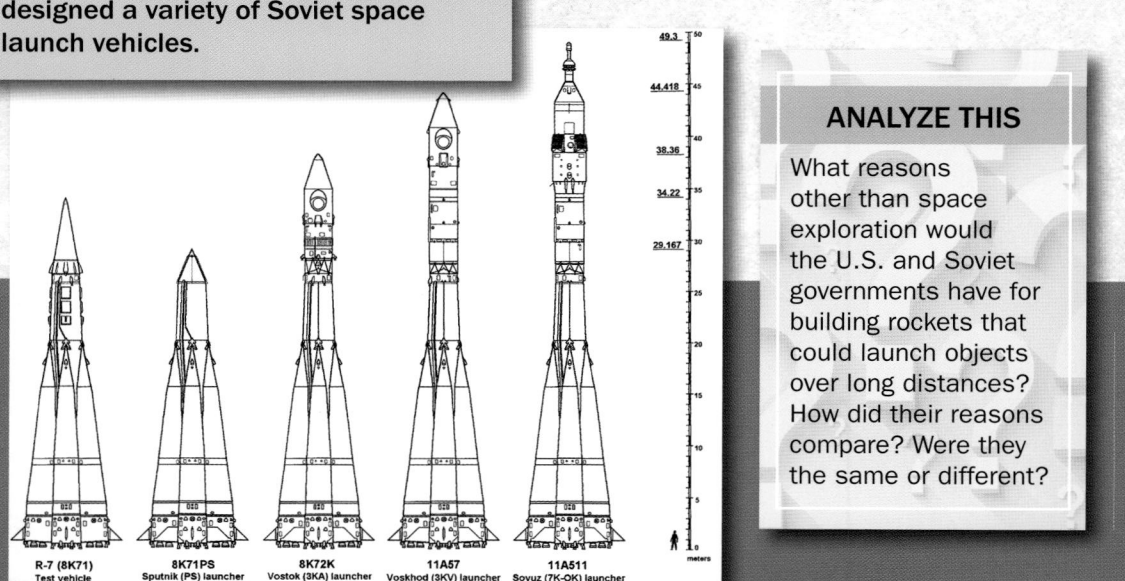

ANALYZE THIS

What reasons other than space exploration would the U.S. and Soviet governments have for building rockets that could launch objects over long distances? How did their reasons compare? Were they the same or different?

AFTER THE RACE

"This is the greatest week in the history of the world since Creation."

U.S. President Richard Nixon about the *Apollo 11* crew after they splash landed on the Pacific Ocean on July 24, 1969

After years of competition, the Space Race ended when the United States put a human on the moon. There were five more *Apollo* lunar missions, and in total, 12 astronauts walked on the moon. The Soviets continued their moon mission for several years, but ultimately they failed and began to focus their energies on building space stations instead. In 1971, the *Soyuz 11* mission ended in disaster when the spacecraft depressurized upon reentry, killing the three-person crew. They are the only humans known to have died in space. Despite this, *Soyuz* spacecraft were considered the safest and most reliable for space travel, and they continue to be used today.

As early as 1963, President Kennedy proposed a union between the space programs of the United States and the U.S.S.R., but Soviet leader Nikita Khrushchev rejected it. Finally, in 1972, the two countries did cooperate through the *Apollo–Soyuz* Test Project.

In 1975, an *Apollo* spacecraft carrying three astronauts took off on July 15 and docked two days later with a Soviet *Soyuz* spacecraft carrying two cosmonauts. NASA designed the docking module used to connect the two spacecraft for the nine-day mission. Together, the astronauts and cosmonauts spent two days conducting five joint experiments. The *Apollo–Soyuz* Test Project was a resounding success from the perspective of paving new pathways for space research and also as a step toward repairing the relationship between the United States and the Soviet Union.

▶ Astronaut Thomas P. Stafford and cosmonaut Alexei A. Leonov (bottom) were chosen to take part in the groundbreaking *Apollo–Soyuz* Test Project.

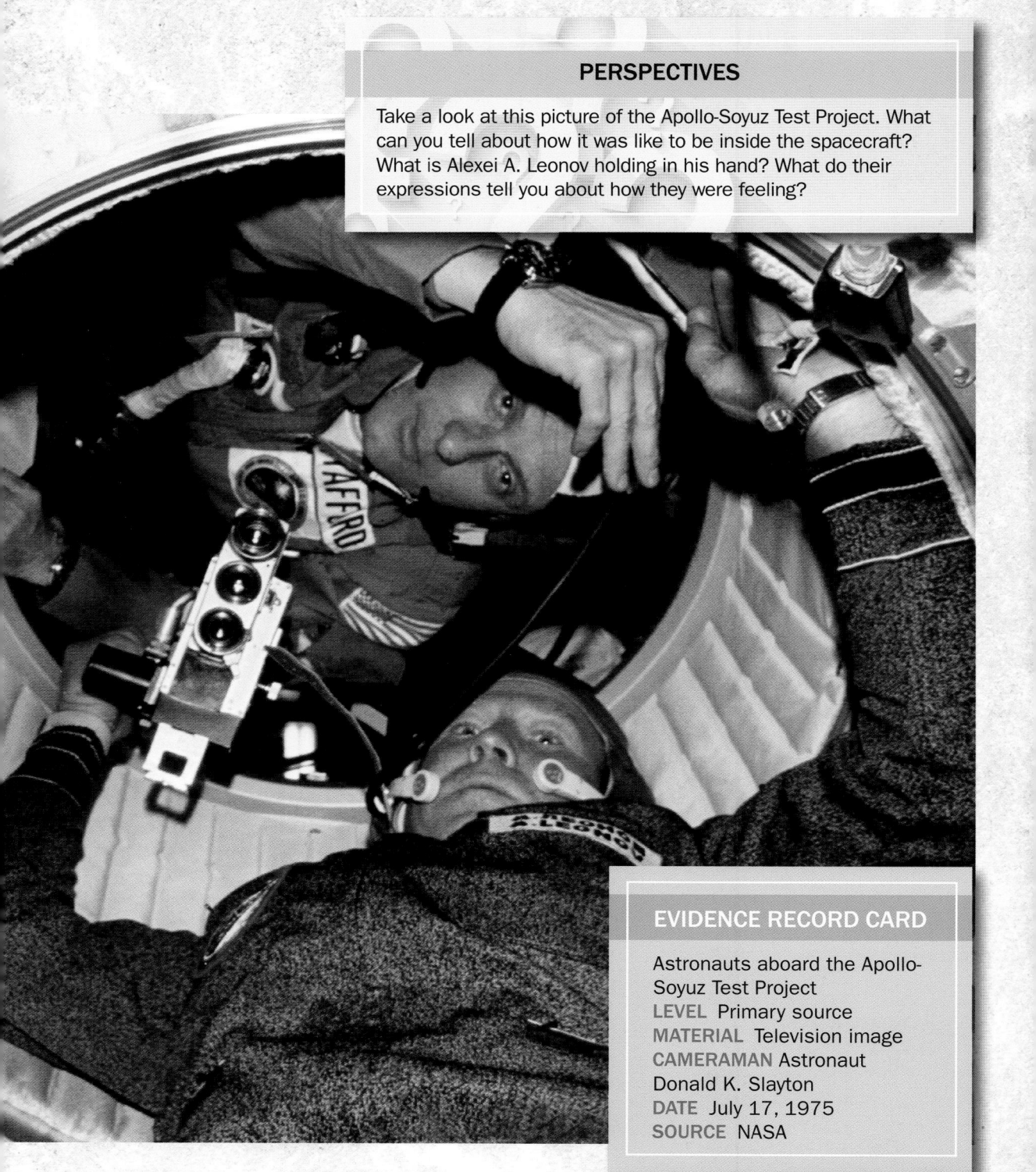

Take a look at this picture of the Apollo-Soyuz Test Project. What can you tell about how it was like to be inside the spacecraft? What is Alexei A. Leonov holding in his hand? What do their expressions tell you about how they were feeling?

EVIDENCE RECORD CARD

Astronauts aboard the Apollo-Soyuz Test Project
LEVEL Primary source
MATERIAL Television image
CAMERAMAN Astronaut Donald K. Slayton
DATE July 17, 1975
SOURCE NASA

END OF AN ERA

With its roots firmly planted in the Cold War, the Space Race had served many purposes. On one hand, both the Americans and the Soviets had wanted to prove they were leaders in scientific research and development. Publicly, both superpowers had proclaimed their research was for the benefit of the general public and improving the lives of everyone.

On the other hand, their research had served a practical, military purpose. Satellites could be used for **reconnaissance** missions and gaining unprecedented information on the other country. Rockets could be used to launch missiles equipped with nuclear bombs. The notion of any one nation gaining a leg up on the other had helped fuel the competition.

▼ **The Outer Space Treaty was created by the United Nations and was signed into effect on October 10, 1967. This primary source sets out rules for all nations regarding space exploration.**

PERSPECTIVES

The Outer Space Treaty bans nations from putting nuclear weapons into orbit and claiming any celestial body as their own. Why do you think these rules were put in place? What other rules would you include in an Outer Space Treaty?

"That's one small step for a man, one giant leap for mankind."

Neil Armstrong, on stepping onto the lunar surface.

MULTILATERAL

Treaty on Principles Governing the Activities of States in the Exploration and Use of Outer Space, Including the Moon and Other Celestial Bodies

Done at Washington, London, and Moscow January 27, 1967;
Ratification advised by the Senate of the United States of America April 25, 1967;
Ratified by the President of the United States of America May 24, 1967;
Ratification of the United States of America deposited at Washington, London, and Moscow October 10, 1967;
Proclaimed by the President of the United States of America October 10, 1967;
Entered into force October 10, 1967.

———

BY THE PRESIDENT OF THE UNITED STATES OF AMERICA
A PROCLAMATION

WHEREAS the Treaty on Principles Governing the Activities of States in the Exploration and Use of Outer Space, including the Moon and Other Celestial Bodies, was signed at Washington, London, and Moscow on January 27, 1967 in behalf of the United States of America, the United Kingdom of Great Britain and Northern Ireland, and the Union of Soviet Socialist Republics and was signed at one or more of the three capitals in behalf of a number of other States;

WHEREAS the text of the Treaty, in the English, Russian, French, Spanish, and Chinese languages, as certified by the Department of State of the United States of America, is word for word as follows:

Rather than fighting for superiority on the battlefield, the United States and the Soviet Union had taken a much less destructive route. But it had still come at a great cost to each nation. From 1961 to 1969, NASA had spent about $23 billion on manned space missions, while the Soviets had invested between $5 billion and $10 billion during the same time.

In the end, having spent about double the money of their rivals, the United States celebrated what they believed was their win, while the Soviets downplayed their perceived defeat. U.S. astronauts from the days of the Space Race went on to become some of the most celebrated heroes in history, while the Soviet cosmonauts were typically portrayed by the American media as the enemy for their constant efforts to best their rivals. Regardless of the outcome of the Space Race, both nations made incredible leaps in science and technology during this period in history and are still world leaders in this area today.

ANALYZE THIS

Do you think the Space Race is over? If so, which country do you consider the winner and why? Has the cost of the race financially and in lives lost been worthwhile? Do the United States and Russia—the modern representation of the Soviet Union—compete in the same way now?

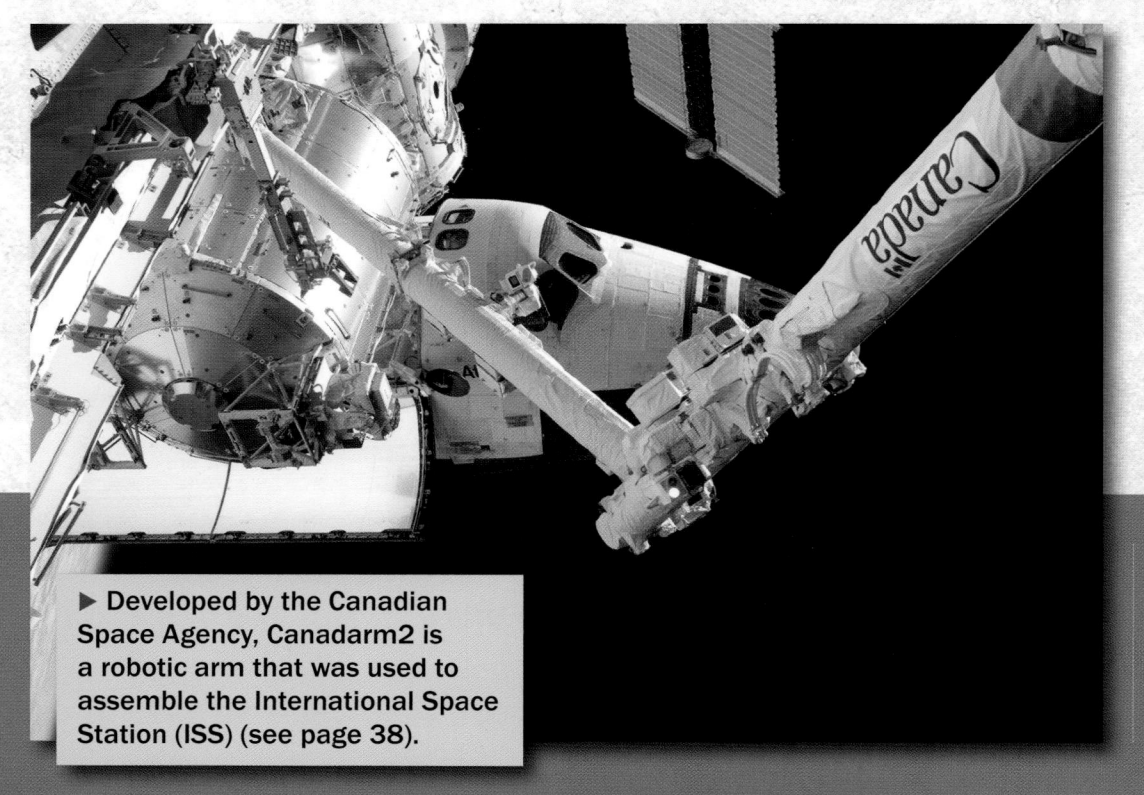

▶ Developed by the Canadian Space Agency, Canadarm2 is a robotic arm that was used to assemble the International Space Station (ISS) (see page 38).

HISTORY REPEATED

"We rely on each other literally for our lives, so despite any political differences our countries may have, or past history, we get along just great."

Mark Kelly, American astronaut in an interview from the International Space Station

ANALYZE THIS

Why do you think other countries wanted to get involved in building the ISS? What contributions do they make to the space program?

With the development of the Space Shuttle—a reusable spacecraft that could make more than one mission into orbit—the United States continued to explore beyond Earth's atmosphere. Between 1981 and 2011, NASA's five Space Shuttles made 135 missions into space. Today, NASA is focusing its attention on exploring farther into space, with its sights on Mars and Jupiter in particular. With an annual budget of nearly $20 billion, the space agency is developing the powerful Space Launch System rocket to carry astronauts all the way to Mars aboard the *Orion* spacecraft.

Beyond that, the Transiting Exoplanet Survey Satellite (*TESS*), launching in 2018, will look outside our solar system in search of other planets and stars.

Following the Space Race, the Soviets maintained their focus on developing orbiting space laboratories. They launched the world's first space station, *Salyut 1*, in 1971, and over the next nine years they placed several variations of the station high above Earth. On February 20, 1986, the U.S.S.R sent a new space station, *Mir*, into orbit, where it remained an active research center for the next 14 years.

In 2011, the International Space Station (ISS) was completed. At the start of its construction in 1998, the ISS was mainly a U.S. and Russian endeavor. However, other countries soon came on board the project. Canada, Japan, Brazil, and 11 members of the European Space Agency played an active role in the development of the ISS. Space travel and exploration had become a truly international effort.

PERSPECTIVES

Take a look at this image of the ISS. What do you see? What type of work do you think happens inside the ISS? How does this work help improve the lives of people around the world?

◀ This photograph of the International Space Station (ISS) was taken from the Space Shuttle Orbiter *Discovery* on August 20, 2001, after it separated from the ISS and returned to Earth.

THE TWENTY-FIRST CENTURY SPACE RACE

In Asia, a new space race is taking place between nations. India, China, and Japan are each developing newer, more improved technologies in a bid to be the first country to reach Mars, deep space, and beyond. They are using their advanced space programs to push a sense of nationalism among their people.

In 2017, India launched a record-breaking 104 satellites from a single rocket. The country has even bigger, bolder plans for 2018, including a mission to the moon. Similarly, China has made promises to bring back a soil sample from the far side of the moon by the end of 2018, and put a space station in orbit by 2022. While Japan had a big setback in its program with the failed launch of one of the world's smallest rockets, it can't be counted out of the race. Japan still has plans for putting an unmanned rover on the moon in 2018.

In recent years, major players in the main Space Race have not been national organizations and their governments but businesspeople and private teams. Unlike publicly funded programs that focus on space exploration and weapons technology, entrepreneurs like Jeff Bezos, Richard Branson, and Elon Musk are looking to send ordinary citizens into space. Their companies, Blue Origin, Virgin Galactic, and SpaceX respectively, are investing in the concept of space tourism. The plan is to send paying passengers into space in the same way that airlines fly travelers around the world. Many well-known celebrities and billionaire business owners are already lining up to pay the hefty fees associated with space flight. It seems only a matter of time before space tourism becomes a reality.

"The Soviets won 3 to 1. The Soviets launched the first Sputnik, the first man in space, the first manned space station…Americans have one victory: The man on the moon."

Sergei Khrushchev, son of former Soviet premier Nikita Khrushchev

▲ *Shenzhou VII*, launched on September 25, 2008, was China's third manned space mission. As part of the mission, Zhai Zhigang became China's first astronaut to complete a spacewalk.

ANALYZE THIS

How is the work the ISRO (see below) is doing important to space exploration? Can other countries around the world benefit from it?

▲ On November 5, 2013, the Indian Space Research Organization (ISRO) launched the Mars Orbiter Mission. ISRO scientists monitored the mission from a command center in Bengaluru, India.

PERSPECTIVES

What is happening in this picture? What does it tell us about the modern-day Space Race?

""*The pace of progress on Mars depends upon the pace of progress of SpaceX.*"
Elon Musk, inventor, engineer, and CEO of Tesla cars and SpaceX

TIMELINE

1917 Communists lead two uprisings against the leaders of Russia, and eventually take power over the country.

August 1949 Soviet Union explodes its first atomic bomb.

July 1955 The United States announces plans to launch a small satellite into space. The Soviets announce similar plans four days later.

December 6, 1957 The U.S. Vanguard Project explodes on live television.

July 29, 1958 U.S. President Eisenhower signs the National Aeronautics and Space Act into effect.

1959 The *Ranger* program begins with the goal of sending spacecraft to the moon.

1961 President John F. Kennedy declares the nation will put a man on the moon by the end of the decade.

January 26, 1962 *Ranger 3* launches into orbit, but it misses the moon.

February 1962 Astronaut John Glenn becomes the first American in orbit.

1964 to 1966 Twelve U.S. Gemini missions take place.

1917

1950

1960

1965

1919 A series of strikes break out in the United States, triggering the First Red Scare.

1953 Soviet chief engineer Sergei Korolev unveils the R-7, the world's first intercontinental ballistic missile with a range of 4,350 miles (7,001 km).

October 4, 1957 The Soviets send the *Sputnik 1* satellite into space. It goes silent after 21 days in space.

January 31, 1958 The first successful American satellite, *Explorer 1*, is carried into space by a Jupiter-C rocket.

September 14, 1959 The Soviets send the *Luna 2* spacecraft to the moon. *Luna 3* flies by the moon nearly a month later.

April 12, 1961 Soviet cosmonaut Yuri Gagarin becomes the first person in space.

1961 to 1968 Saturn launch vehicles send several unmanned Apollo spacecraft into orbit.

1964 The Soviets launch the *Voskhod 1* for two missions.

1965 The Soviets fly *Voskhod 2* on two missions.

April 1967 The Soviets launch a manned crew into space, but a parachute failure results in the death of a cosmonaut.

1971 The *Soyuz 11* mission ends in disaster, killing the three-person crew.

1972 The United States and the Soviet Union negotiate an agreement to work together in space.

1981 to 2011 NASA's five Space Shuttles make 135 missions into space.

1965

2011

October 1966 The first unmanned *Soyuz* mission takes place.

1968 The first successful manned *Soyuz* mission takes place.

July 20, 1969 The United States lands an astronaut on the moon. Neil Armstrong and Buzz Aldrin take their first steps on the lunar surface.

1975 The United States and Soviet Union team up for the *Apollo–Soyuz* Test Project.

2011 Construction finishes on the International Space Station (ISS).

World map showing active space-research launch sites

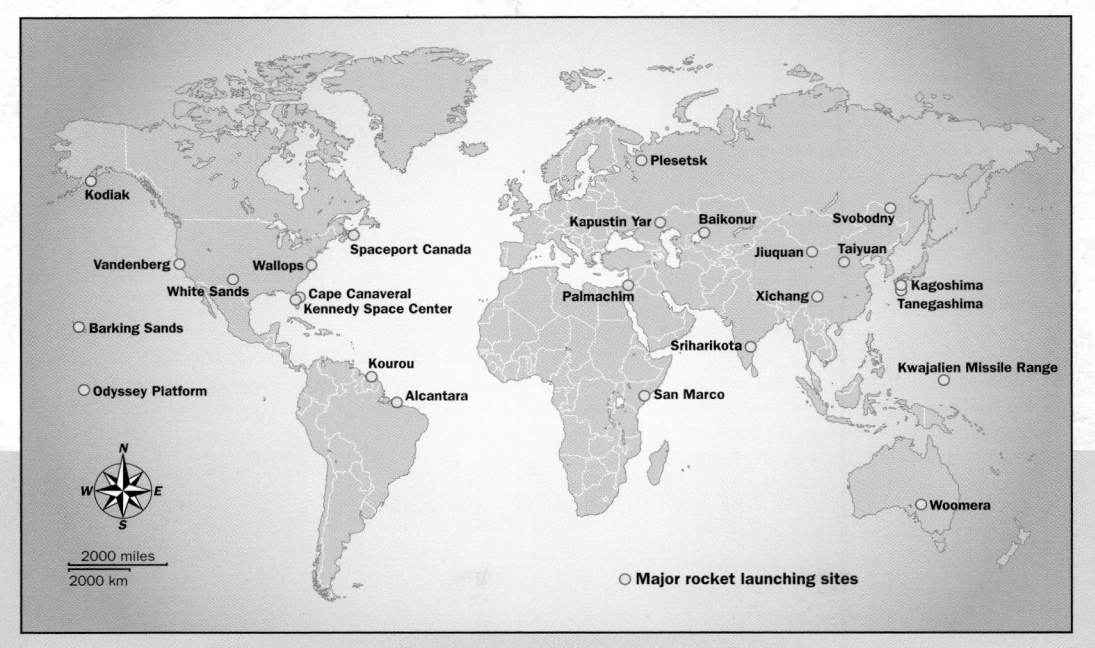

Kodiak
Plesetsk
Kapustin Yar
Baikonur
Svobodny
Vandenberg
Wallops
Spaceport Canada
Jiuquan
Taiyuan
White Sands
Cape Canaveral
Kennedy Space Center
Palmachim
Xichang
Kagoshima
Tanegashima
Barking Sands
Sriharikota
Kourou
Kwajalien Missile Range
Odyssey Platform
Alcantara
San Marco
N
W E
S
Woomera
2000 miles
2000 km
○ Major rocket launching sites

BIBLIOGRAPHY

QUOTATIONS

P. 4 Socrates as reported by Plato. Northeast Kingdom Astronomy Foundation, Capturing Starlight, 2017. http://www.nkaf.org/

P. 6 Johnson, Lyndon B. Speech at the American Rocket Society, October 13, 1961. https://er.jsc.nasa.gov/seh/quotes.html

P. 8 Mead, Margaret. Chabot College, Astronomy Worksheet, 2017. https://www.chabotcollege.edu/faculty/shildreth/astronomy/NASA2016.html

P. 10 Kennedy, John F. Address at Rice University on the Space Effort, September 12, 1962. http://explore.rice.edu/explore/kennedy_address.asp

P. 14 Shetterly, Margo Lee. *Hidden Figures: The American Dream and the Untold Story of the Black Women Mathematicians Who Helped Win the Space Race.* William Morrow and Company, 2016.

P. 16 Lovell, Jim. New Mexico Museum of Space History, International Space Hall of Fame, 2017. http://www.nmspacemuseum.org/halloffame/detail.php?id=65

P. 19 Kennedy, John F. John F. Address at Rice University on the Space Effort, September 12, 1962. http://explore.rice.edu/explore/kennedy_address.asp

P. 20 Bradbury, Ray. Interview with Ken Kelley. raybradbury.com, 2017. http://www.raybradbury.com/articles_playboy.html

P. 23 Sagan, Carl. *Pale Blue Dot: A Vision of the Human Future in Space.* Random House Publishing, 1994.

P. 24 Khrushchev, Sergei. "The Moon Landing through Soviet Eyes: A Q&A with Sergei Khrushchev, son of former premier Nikita Khrushchev." Scientific American, July 16, 2009. https://www.scientificamerican.com/article/apollo-moon-khrushchev/

P. 26 Gagarin Yuri. "Great Quotes." Today in Space History, 2017. https://todayinspacehistory.wordpress.com/great-quotes/

P. 29 Khrushchev, Nikita. AZ Quotes, 2017. http://www.azquotes.com/quote/1122597— Nikita

P. 31 Goddard, Robert. "Dr. Robert H. Goddard, American Rocketry Pioneer." NASA, 2017. https://www.nasa.gov/centers/goddard/about/history/dr_goddard.html

P. 32 Rees, Martin. BrainyQuote, 2017. https://www.brainyquote.com/quotes/quotes/m/martinrees564054.html

P. 34 Nixon, Richard. Remarks to *Apollo 11* Astronauts Aboard the U.S.S. *Hornet* Following Completion of Their Lunar Mission, July 24, 1969. http://www.presidency.ucsb.edu/ws/?pid=2138

P. 36 Armstrong, Neil. Remarks during the moon landing, July 20, 1969. https://www.nasa.gov/mission_pages/apollo/apollo11.html

P. 38 Kelly, Mark. "How historic handshake in space brought superpowers closer." CNN, July 15, 2015. http://www.cnn.com/2015/07/15/world/space-handshake-anniversary/index.html

P. 40 Khrushchev, Sergei. "Astronaut, Soviet's Son Argue Space Race." The Associated Press, October 4, 2007. http://www.washingtonpost.com/wp-dyn/content/article/2007/10/04/AR2007100402671_pf.html

P. 41 Musk, Elon. "Musk says under 5 percent of SpaceX is working on Mars mission, 2024 launch is 'optimistic'." TechCrunch, September 27, 2016. https://techcrunch.com/2016/09/27/musk-says-under-5-percent-of-spacex-is-working-on-mars-mission-2024-launch-is-optimistic/

TO FIND OUT MORE

Abadzis, Nick. *Laika*. Missouri: Turtleback Books, 2007.

Benoit, Peter. *The Space Race.* New York: Scholastic, 2012.

Hubbard, Ben. *Yuri Gagarin and the Race to Space.* New Hampshire: Heinemann, 2016.

McGowen, Tom. *Space Race: The Mission, the Men, the Moon.* New Jersey: Enslow Publishers, 2009.

Paris, Stephanie. *20th Century: Race to the Moon.* California: TIME FOR KIDS Nonfiction Readers, 2013.

Shetterly, Margot Lee. *Hidden Figures.* New York: William Morrow Books, 2016.

Turkina, Olesya. *Soviet Space Dogs.* London: FUEL Publishing, 2014.

Wood, Matthew Brenden. *The Space Race: How the Cold War Put Humans on the Moon.* Vermont: Nomad Press, 2018.

INTERNET GUIDELINES

Finding good source material on the Internet can sometimes be a challenge. When analyzing how reliable the information is, consider these points:

- Who is the author of the page? Is it an expert in the field or a person who experienced the event?
- Is the site well known and up to date? A page that has not been updated for several years probably has out-of-date information.
- Can you verify the facts with another site? Always double-check information.

- Have you checked all possible sites? Don't just look on the first page a search engine provides. Remember to try government sites and research papers.
- Have you recorded website addresses and names? Keep this data so you can backtrack and verify the information you want to use.

WEBSITES:

NASA: A Brief History of Animals in Space
Read about the animals that took part in the Space Race.
https://history.nasa.gov/animals.html

Canadian Space Agency Timeline: Canadian Space Milestones
Find out how Canada has contributed to space exploration and research throughout history.
http://www.asc-csa.gc.ca/eng/about/milestones.asp

John F. Kennedy Presidential Library and Museum: Space Program
Learn all about President Kennedy's role in the Space Race.
https://www.jfklibrary.org/JFK/JFK-in-History/Space-Program.aspx

John F. Kennedy Presidential Library and Museum: Americans in Space
Check out a variety of primary source materials from the Space Race.
https://www.jfklibrary.org/Education/Students/Americans-in-Space.aspx

Smithsonian National Air and Space Museum: Space Race
Learn all about the space rivalry between the United States and the Soviet Union.
https://airandspace.si.edu/exhibitions/space-race

Ducksters: The Cold War Space Race
Find out more about the events of the Cold War and Space Race missions.
http://www.ducksters.com/history/cold_war/space_race.php

Canadian Aviation and Space Museum: Library and Archives
Research the Space Race using this comprehensive database of information.
https://ingeniumcanada.org/aviation/collection-research/library-archives.php

Encyclopedia Britannica: Space Exploration
Learn about space research and exploration throughout history.
https://www.britannica.com/topic/space-exploration

GLOSSARY

accurate Correct in all details

aerospace The branch of science and technology that focuses on aviation and space flight

affiliations People or organizations that are connected to larger organizations

Allies Nations, such as Britain, France, Canada, the United States, and the Soviet Union, that fought together against Germany during World War I and World War II

analyze Examine closely

archives Places that store historical information about a location, a person, or an event

Arms Race A competition between nations to have the most powerful military force; in particular, the nuclear arms race between the United States and the U.S.S.R

arsenal A collection of weapons, arms, and military equipment

artifacts Objects made by human beings

auditory Related to the sense of hearing

balanced Judged or presented in a way that is fair and takes all views into account

biased Prejudiced in favor of or against one thing, person, or group

capitalism An economic and political system in which trade and industry are privately owned

century A period of 100 years

citizens People who have full rights to live in a country

Cold War The worldwide political, economic, and military confrontation between the United States, the Soviet Union, and their allies that lasted from 1946 to 1991

communist An economic and political system in which all property is owned by its members and is used for the good of all people

credentials Qualifications or achievements

credible Something that can be believed

culture The ideas, customs, traditions, and behavior of a people

decades Periods of ten years

disillusioned Disappointed by something that is not as good as was originally believed

economic Having to do with creating, earning, and spending wealth

evaluate Judge the value of something

evidence The information or facts that indicate whether something is true or not

generations All the people born and living at the same time

intercontinental ballistic missiles Missiles that can be propelled more than 3,400 miles (5,500 km)

International Geophysical Year A global science project that ran from July 1, 1957 to December 31, 1958

ionosphere The layer of the atmosphere that is about 50 to 600 miles (80 to 965 km) above Earth's surface

media Plural of medium; medium is one way of expressing an idea and includes the press, TV, and radio

missile Object that is forcefully thrown at target

NASA The U.S. National Aeronautics and Space Administration

patriotism Love or devotion for one's country

payload Cargo

perspectives Points of view or ways of looking at something

premier In the U.S.S.R, the head of government

primary source A firsthand account or direct evidence of an event

propaganda Information, often misleading or biased, used to promote a particular point of view

prosecuting Taking legal action against someone

reconnaissance Survey an area to gather information about it

redoubled Made something greater or more intense

revolution A use of force to overthrow a government

rockets Powered vehicles used for carrying satellites and spacecraft into space

satellites Human-made objects sent into orbit around planets and celestial bodies

secondary sources Materials created by studying primary sources

societies Groups of people forming a single community with its own distinctive culture and institutions

source materials Original documents or other pieces of evidence

spies People employed by a government or other organization to secretly obtain information about an enemy or competitor

strikes Protests that involve refusing to work

subversive Seeking to overthrow, destroy, or undermine an existing or established system

tertiary sources An account made by analyzing and interpreting a combination of primary and secondary sources

World War I War fought from 1914 to 1918 between the United States, Canada, the United Kingdom, France, Italy, Japan, and their allies against Germany, Austria-Hungary, the Ottoman Empire (Turkey), and their allies: The United States entered the war in 1917.

World War II War fought from 1939 to 1945 between the United States, Canada, Britain, the U.S.S.R, and their allies against Nazi Germany, Italy, Japan, and their allies: The United States, U.S.S.R, and Japan entered the war in 1941.

INDEX

28 DAY BOOK
Hewlett-Woodmere Public Library
Hewlett, New York 11557

Business Phone 516-374-1967
Recorded Announcements 516-374-1667
Website www.hwpl.org